My Words Healed My Soul

Keya S. McClain

Copyright © 2016 Keya S. McClain
All rights reserved.

ISBN: 1530916259
ISBN 13: 9781530916252

My sincere thanks extends to all my family and friends who supported my work and journey. When I started writing as a child, I never knew it would transform into the art that it has. To all the poets I encountered that inspired me and the very special ones that welcomed me, I am honored to be able to share my work with each of you. To some very close jewels that pushed me to keep performing and never let my light go out: my mom, who has always been my biggest fan; and my sister-friends who are more like my family. My brother-friends who are loving, protective, and very encouraging. I am hopeful that you will take your time to allow the words to resonate with you and penetrate the deepest part of your soul in some way. Writing became my alternate trip to the couch if I couldn't make it there. As life happened, words remained the same and the way the words pierced my very soul became the way I healed. Even the joy and silly personality shines through a few of the poems and stories. A very special thank-you to my mother Deborah Miller, my sisters Shalonda Laurel and Trish McClain-Garner, my brother in poetry, Floyd Boykin Jr., my longtime friend and brother Jermaine Tart, sister-friends Tenille Rose Martin, Patrice Willis, Tori Smith, Tawanna Watson, Denise Pearson, Alex Stallings,

Vivian Johnson, Aretha Pruitt, Sherita Calhoun, Shauntae Noel-Al Hejoj, Melanie Mckenzie, Carmen Jefferson Steward, my dear friend Kelvin Adams, my cousin Keyon Love, the ladies of Empower2Be, my son Corey A. Harris Jr., nephews Bryon C. Haynes and Corey Hayes and niece Tanija Carter. There are so many others I can name, and my gratitude for each person who supported, encouraged, impacted me, and prayed for me to complete this can never be shown enough. I am humble, honored, and thankful for the gift God has blessed me with and even more that you are willing to take the journey with me.

Contents

OUR LOVE	8
CONDOLENCES	10
EVERY MAN'S DREAM	11
TO WHOM IT MAY CONCERN	13
SUMMER TRIPS	16
MY TRUE LOVE	17
THE END	19
THE JOURNEY	21
PUSHING	23
LIFER	25
CONSEQUENCES	27
CONTEMPLATING	28
ARRIVED	30
MY BROTHER	32

IN REMEMBRANCE OF ALL OF YOU 34

PMS 36

NOT MUCH HAS CHANGED 40

MY HAIR 43

I WRITE 45

CARPET RIDE 47

BOOK TITLE 48

SHE MATTERED 50

BATTERED AND BRUISED 51

HIGH 52

CONFUSED LOVE 53

I DON'T MIND 54

INVITE 56

THANK GOD FOR MY DAYS 57

JUST LIKE THAT 58

THIS IS MY LIFE 59

WEB OF LIES 61

SEE YOU 62

BLOODSTAINED PAVEMENT 63

PAIN IN HER EYES 65

KINDRED SPIRITS 67

THE TRUTH 69

PURPOSE 70

INGREDIENTS TO LIFE 72

THE AWARD GOES TO YOU 73

YOUR ASSUMPTIONS 74

WITHDRAWAL 76

MY TEARS 77

PRAISE FOR KEYA'S WORK 79

OUR LOVE

Intentionally inhaling and exhaling as to not inhale your present scent and love until I fall into a coma.

The vibration of your heart as I lean in toward your embrace.

And just to taste the softness of your lips.

The way you guide me closer to your face.

The way your eyes sparkle at the sight of me.

The octaves in your voice from complimentary to a soft yet firm tone.

The way you love God and honor what He has blessed you with without regrets.

The sacrifices I have yet to see but know will take place.

As we find our way in this new and amazing space.

Feeling closer to you as each day passes.

And knowing there is a such thing as happily ever after.

Because our love…our love is like a well-blended tea.

And we are certain to maintain this level of chemistry.

You know that kind—where you are bound to drop to one knee.

Confessing your love and desire for a lifelong mate.

We've agreed to always date.

Always forgive.

And completely live.

Live a life full of romance.

Because it's no longer taking a chance.

We've committed to this…this lifelong dance.

CONDOLENCES

I've come to pay my condolences on today.

The dash on my headstone will read: Born May 4, with two dashes.

The first dash reflects the awakening.

Therefore, the old me had to be laid to rest and a new life created.

Just as the caterpillar turns into a butterfly.

This life has gone through stages to birth the newly developed me.

In this new life, I can't care if you like me or not.

Neither am I concerned about, nor will I entertain your bad behavior.

Knowing and realizing I won't be everyone's flavor.

There is no need to sit around and attempt to savor.

I have said my good-byes and began to emerge.

And just like a bird, I've learned how to fly.

You may now say your final good-bye.

EVERY MAN'S DREAM

She is every man's dream,

her skin a perfect blend of all the browns, with oval-shaped wide eyes.

Her walk is hypnotic, and her words flow out like the slow drippings of honey in a low and seductive tone.

Men can't help but to stop and stare.

Some feed her the sweetest and subtlest compliments, while others yell and scream,

Taunt and point at her, making her feel the most uncomfortable feeling.

And no matter how many times she hears it—You're beautiful—

She can't help but to pick herself apart from the lines on her face to the shape of her toes.

She is sweet yet seductive.

She's always used her sexiness as a last resort.

It's often after hearing some man confess his desire to spend an entire fortune on her.

That lack of esteem seems to dissipate, if only temporarily, to work her magic.

She knows how to use her words and her eyes to get what she likes.

He isn't aware of this fact.

In fact, his last comment implies just that.

She doesn't stand a chance with neither woman nor man.

While the men adore and revel, the women snarl and avoid her.

Most don't understand her gentle and kind touch.

Her desire to love and be loved.

To shine a light that has nothing to do with her physical appearance, just the love she has inside.

For most, they don't know that she wants to see them succeed, support, and acknowledge and provide them a balance.

An all-around looker, they say, without ever knowing what she holds within.

So she really doesn't care if she's every man's dream.

TO WHOM IT MAY CONCERN

This serves as my resignation.

There is no reason to give notice.

No two-week notice, no few days' notice.

You've been warned.

I've expressed my desire to be treated a certain way.

You've been given a probationary period that you couldn't complete.

Your attitude and actions have shown me just how much you didn't want this position.

It is clear to me that you didn't read or comprehend the job description.

Let me be clear; I know I'm not perfect, and I too have flaws.

However, my flaws are open like a new cut or wound.

I can understand you wanting the position and feeling qualified.

I too have had aspirations of applying before qualified.

I have taken the time to study though.

I concentrated on me and learned to understand who I was and, more important, who I am.

It is also important that I express my disappointment in your lies in your interview.

The way you answered questions and even your references were all deceitful.

As management, it is partly my fault…you see, I realized I did not do a thorough background investigation.

Nor did I pay close enough attention to the signs of your disqualification early on.

The inconsistences and failure to improve over time.

There should always be increase, better work product, and growth in any position.

At the review process, I usually marked "needs improvement" or "satisfactory."

I do not believe this is an acceptable rating.

Since your last review consists of "needs improvement" or "no growth at all in this area," I'm afraid this position is no longer available.

I resign from the position of being your friend, your lover, your family member, or your acquaintance.

I have been committed, loyal, and loving toward you.

I may have made some mistakes, and I may have also even failed at some things.

In this position that I've held with you though, it is over, complete, finished.

There is not one bit of love lost either.

This, my friend, is good-bye.

No other documentation is needed.

Management!

SUMMER TRIPS

Bags are packed, and goodies are stacked.

As Granny tells us to keep our behavior intact.

The stomachache I have is not from anything other than excitement over the road trip Granny has planned.

Waving to friends and trying to stand really long because the ride is sometimes bumpy and certainly fun

Watching the cows and horses out the window is our sign that we aren't far.

Gravel roads and winding roads means we've hit the town.

And as we hit Angular Road in Clinton, Kentucky, we know we are in for some fun.

But not so happy about basking in the southern sun.

MY TRUE LOVE

I've clearly crossed the line here.

Allowing my mind to escape in this place where our hands have interlocked, the beats of our hearts match, and the world has completely come to a halt.

The world as I knew it just doesn't exist anymore.

I've succumbed to the desires of your touch.

I'm dancing on the tippy-toes of love.

Allowing my hand to trace the outline of my heart as it makes a beautiful, melodic sound that only you can create.

It is clear this is right because I used to hesitate.

Hesitate at obliging at your every advance.

When, finally, my heart just had to take a stance.

I have made it clear to you and everyone else that I've finally chosen you.

I am no longer teetering on the sidelines watching everyone else's glow.

It is time for me to have life's rewards and continue to grow.

In my long time admiration of you, I always failed at getting to intimately know you.

Taking time to sit quietly and alone with just you.

Making promises to date you eventually.

Preparing trips and even quiet time, just me and you.

And although I really wanted to make you number one,

And admit you are second to none,

I had to take this journey to meet you again.

Creating lasting memories and demonstrating how your love has changed me.

Defining your love in a new and greater height.

I've learned to appreciate and love everything about you.

From your thick lips to your wide hips.

To your long locs and that stride in your walk.

Even the wide and amazing smile you have that catches the world's eyes.

You are a simply amazing love.

A true, devoted, and loyal love.

The love I've always wanted and searched for.

I truly thank God for blessing me with her.

My true love for self.

THE END

In that place where loss has a way of sitting heavily on my chest.

Silencing my screams.

Deleting every single future dream.

And facing the undeniable truth of gone, loss, and I can't see you anymore.

Hear your voice and the laugher we all loved so.

Without even a warning or get ready, I'm gone.

This space that I'm in gets more closed in.

The baffling trend that we are all coming to our end.

It's a huge level of weight to even contemplate.

For me more so because I just want to live the life God intended for me.

Being sure that my dash will be far more memorable than the date at the end.

That my family and friends won't forget how I lived and I laughed.

How I used words and my fist in my earlier years.

Only to avoid the downpour of tears.

But learned to shift that to paper and pen.

We all know that feeling of destruction and lost.

Despite what you believe, it can be at the highest cost.

The violence, the cancer, and even when there's no answer.

Remember how quick life can be snatched.

Because there is no way to avoid… The End.

THE JOURNEY

The black and gray suits.

Multicolored ties.

And mixture of staring eyes.

I feel completely out of my element.

But knowing my journey is just beginning.

The hard work is finally paying off.

All those long hours and college courses have gotten me there.

I remember as a child dreaming of this time.

The time where I would be wearing my suit and heels.

And not spinning my wheels.

Trying to determine what I wanted to be. Who I wanted to be and how I needed to be.

The journey was long and sometimes hard, so I encourage you to:

Continue to push through,

Continue to know who you are,

Continue to believe,

Because in the end you will succeed.

Our journeys are meaningful.

Your story will hold the key to another's journey

PUSHING

When you reach that plateau.

Knowing you have taken yourself so far.

Reaching for the stars.

Yet complacency and stagnation has taken up residency.

And you've stayed behind that fence for way too long.

It is time to set a brand-new tone.

While climbing to be in a different zone.

Don't continue to do it alone.

The time to be brave is now.

Set yourself completely apart.

You are the epitome of a Braveheart.

Strong and resilient.

But pushing to be more persistent and consistent.

Establishing your team while building your dream.

And holding yourself accountable for nurturing your self-esteem.

Because you know where you plan to be.

And the goals you expect to achieve.

So place yourself at the highest expectation.

Push past the fear.

Drive faster as you look to the rear.

Your dreams do not expire.

The highest form of dreams may lead you to perspire.

But I implore you to continue to reach higher.

LIFER

The next and final lifer will get the full advantage of not being cut by the various broken pieces of me.

I will also reap the benefits of getting the one who is healed and won't receive any cuts or punctures from him.

This lifer and I are sure to win.

He will see my healed scars, and I will see his.

We will place our gentle and loving hands over those scars with tenderness and great care.

Our love will be real, whole, and we will come bare.

The stitches have been put in by God, and I feel the continuous peace and healing.

I wish I could describe the depth of this feeling.

There's no denying the hurt and pain we've both endured.

But we are each other's lifers, and there's no denying that.

Our previous pain will not hinder our love.

In fact, it has helped us to rely on God up above.

We've entered this with trust, forgiveness, loyalty, and endless love.

Why shouldn't we have all that we deserve?

I'm just thankful that you are my final lifer.

And you told your family, "I just have to wife her."

CONSEQUENCES

Consequences of your choices will inevitably come.

You will miss the lessons and the blessings if you do not succumb.

Succumb to the guidance and wisdom from up above and, equally important, what you hold within.

Encamping yourself around nothing but love.

Allowing forgiveness and redemption to guide and lead your new way.

Not pointing blame or resentment toward anyone specifically.

Just allowing healing and wisdom to create new space.

Terminate all your past poor choices and live in the now.

Because no one or nothing else determines your future.

Stand tall and proud about how far you've come.

You could still be that person who made nothing but bad choices.

Your life is your own, and you're already on the throne.

We were all made to be kings and queens.

Be not discouraged about yesterday.

For the real tragedy is in continued delay.

CONTEMPLATING

It's a quarter past nine, and I'm still contemplating.

Still contemplating on the moment.

The moment when I slit my wrist or take those pills or load that clip.

I've been dying inside for so long that I may as well pull that trigger—I may as well pierce that artery, and I may as well drift into that sleep that does not awaken me.

But I'm awake right now, right?

I'm thinking and speaking and feeling and needing.

That's it.

I've instantly revived myself, and it didn't take a push to the chest or a breath to my breath to do this.

Do what? Because I'm numb again.

I have no feeling on my left side, and I feel like maybe I've had a stroke or maybe I've choked.

Choked on the smoke that has filled my lungs.

The smoke that has filled my lungs that prevents any breath.

Breath to breathe, breath to live, breath to…breath.

I can't move. and my body is certainly numb.

I'm numb; I mean, I'm so numb I feel like I'm paralyzed from the waist down.

My arms are moving, my fingers are moving, and my head is moving.

Below I am numb though.

I have shut that part off.

That part that has caused me to feel this way.

That part of the body that has caused this pain.

I've been exposed and now everyone knows that I hurt like they hurt.

And I endure pain like they endure pain.

My pulse is getting weak, and it's getting harder to speak.

Harder to speak about the pain I've sustained and the tears that I've cried…and the torture.

The torture.

Some self-inflicted wounds…wounds that have healed and others that have turned into ugly scars.

But right now…I'm still contemplating.

ARRIVED

I've purposely arrived here.

I wasn't misguided or misled by any GPS or map.

In fact, I didn't need directions at all.

The sign read: danger ahead.

I proceeded as if it read "caution."

Proceeded as if there would be no repercussions.

Be no repercussions for proceeding ahead.

And as much fear as I had, it should have deterred me from moving into that head-on collision.

And although I had fear, there was still that curiosity to keep going to see where that road would lead me.

As I continued on this road, I was introduced to anger, animosity, and fear.

Hatred and envy soon became acquaintances of mine.

And after becoming familiar with them, I moved on to betrayal and deceit.

I then stumbled upon the cheaters and liars.

Now the impact of the collision is felt by many.

The collision that could have been prevented with some logic and reason.

I sit here wondering how I arrived in this place.

How I kept going when I could tell that this road was full of darkness and pain.

Bitterness and failure, so I sit in my quiet place, meditating and praying and then realizing I was led here.

Led here on a spiritual journey, hence the caution sign ahead, no danger ahead, realizing this journey has landed me to my destination.

The land of peace, tranquility, and solace.

Because things had been so imbalanced for all this time that I hadn't realized

I'd arrived.

MY BROTHER

At introduction the words used to describe you to me were "He's just like you.

You all are sure to hit it off."

These words poured out nearly twenty years before our last meeting, and our very first meeting was just like our very last meeting.

Slick and sly words bounced off walls without ever missing a beat.

A beat.

Heartbeat.

Heartbeats affected by your recent demise, a strong pounding to a nearly flat line.

I was screaming,

Screaming internally and externally too.

This couldn't be true, not my best friend and big brother.

And although the streaming bloodlines of DNA did not match, we were siblings,

Siblings who shared in the joys and the losses,

The birthdays and holidays,

The text or call that said nothing more than "I'm here" or "Let's talk."

But now I'm taking that long walk,

Trying to retrace the steps I took when that phone call came through,

The call that buckled my knees and released all my wind.

Some days, hoping if I retrace those steps I could rewind that time

and I would surely be willing to spend my last dime

To see you, to hear you, to tell you I love you.

But that time has passed, and you are so truly missed.

Each day that passes seems more like a dream.

But I remember the day I felt just like a queen.

When you walked me down the aisle to who I thought was my king.

But with your sense of humor, I'm not surprised at this fact.

Not to mention the friends I've acquired just because of you.

I promise to always remember you and to hold all the memories we shared without much despair, but I miss you.

It was such a short time but how blessed I was to call you my brother.

There definitely won't be another.

IN REMEMBRANCE OF ALL OF YOU

Gasping for air and holding my chest, as the pain is too much to bear.

As I watch this generation lose the values of those before us.

The rights and privileges we have were intensely fought for and blood was shed for the basic rights we have now.

So it's particularly perplexing to me that as a society we continue to sit complacently.

Sit complacently while heartless and heinous acts of violence are committed against our people.

Turning our heads and sticking our heads in the sands as if we are ostriches that refuse to see anything.

And although it is your prerogative to live your life as you choose, we have an obligation as a people to keep our focus on forward-going and positive change.

Prevention and protection from those who don't respect life.

We should all feel dismayed by the propensity of young people to act out violently, without regard and with a great deal of disrespect, and it starts with each of us.

Each of us had someone pray for us or mentor us, and we should be giving back as a whole.

There should be a movement across the world for change.

I'm talking about a change that prevents families from the hurt and pain from losing loved ones.

Change that stops us from blaming the government's inept ability to get involved in our communities, while we step up and change our own communities block by block, person by person.

These are the changes our ancestors fought for, and we must regain this momentum by starting now.

And while it is apparent that some will undoubtedly sit on their hands and watch from the sidelines,

You still have work to do.

A work that is inherently inside of you.

It is time to be deliberate in your steps and faithful in your works, and we can even be diplomatic in this approach by automatically praying to God and asking for deliverance now.

PMS

This morning I felt so happy and alive and grateful and more thankful than ever.

After arriving at work and having my coffee, I felt even better.

By the afternoon that morning smile had dissipated and turned into a frown, and by the end of the day, as I prepared to leave the office, I was ready to scream.

I got in my car, only to be caught in a damn traffic jam that sends me into a straight road rage.

Not my regular road rage—yes, I do have a regular road rage—but the road rage that causes the lines on my head to protrude from under my bangs.

I sit in this traffic jam while switching from radio station to radio station, only to hear some annoying man's voice giving advice to someone who has asked the entire city of Saint Louis to weigh in on his relationship.

The relationship that talks about infidelity, abuse, and neglect.

The man weighs in with his opinion, which leads me to shaking my head,

Shaking my head as he provides a response for the infidelity, abuse, and neglect and blaming the woman and excusing the man.

Just annoyed.

Annoyed with everybody right now, so I start to calculate days in my head because I woke up happy and grateful and my day is quickly turning.

Fourteen, twenty-one, twenty-three, twenty-four—oh damn! PMS is setting in.

Now that I've calculated the days in my head, the bloating suddenly begins, my head hurts, and now I'm annoyed with what that man said to me yesterday, so I decide to pick up my phone and call him to tell him just how stupid I really think he is.

Just as I start to dial, the phone rings, and it's my son, who tells me he left his key in his locker and he's locked outside.

I tell him there is nothing I can do because I'm sitting in a damn traffic jam and he needs to get it together to prepare to be a man. I mean, damn.

He pauses for a few moments, and I hear him say out loud, "Fourteen, twenty-one, twenty-three, twenty-four. OK, Mom. I'll be waiting outside when you arrive. Be safe, and I love you."

As I continue to sit in this traffic jam, the back pain and tension in my shoulders only gets worse.

In less than twelve hours, I've gone from happy to mad, and now I'm feeling real sad.

I finally arrive at home and start to say it's time to calm.

I warm up some water to have a cup of tea,

Only to realize I drank the last cup last week.

Now I'm beyond mad. I'm mad as hell.

I slide my shoes on and decide to run to the store to get some more tea,

Only to find that the express lane is not open, and only two lanes are open at Shop 'n Save."

And damn.

It's Thursday night.

Ten-dollars-off coupon night.

The lady in front of me turns around and smiles at me,

But I'm not feeling like smiling.

In an effort to jump the line, I give her a fake smile,

But Ms. Thang turns back around and starts to load her hundred items on the conveyor belt.

I close my eyes and silently say woo-sah.

After being at Shop 'n Save for thirty-five minutes too long,

I make my way back home

And prepare to make my tea.

Now I can relax and calm down because I'm starting to get madder and even depressed.

I hate when this time comes because my emotions are just so out of whack.

And just as I start to calm down and say, "You only have a few more days,"

Then that have-a-happy-period commercial comes on.

NOT MUCH HAS CHANGED

Not much has changed since the beginning.

The beginning of Me, I mean.

The days where I had to be fed, nurtured, loved, taught, and instructed.

I still have a daily need to have all those things provided and fulfilled.

I need to be fed. Feed Me with all the positive and loving energy that you have.

I need to be nurtured. Nurtured by your attentiveness and gentle touch.

I need to be loved. Love Me like you loved me in the beginning—unconditional love.

I need to be taught. Teach me to continue to walk and stay grounded and confident in that walk.

I need to be instructed. Instruction is essential to continuous knowledge.

But somehow…somehow things got so complicated. You were making plans and attending school and dating and hanging with friends, and yeah, things got complicated.

In the beginning I was so happy about all the love and attention you gave Me. It showed in the gifts from you to Me, and I noticed the change in the frequency and the attention to My needs, and you slowly drifted away from Me.

I started to believe it was Me and that I had to do something different, or maybe you needed something different from Me. When all this time I had been giving you what I thought was all you needed, and that was Me.

I gave you My love and when you were lonely, I was there and when you cried, I wiped your tears and when you fell on your knees, I was on My knees right beside you.

When you hurt, I felt the pain. When someone did you wrong, I felt as though they did Me wrong.

Yet you turned your back, felt the need to walk away from Me. Initially, I felt that you would come back, and I felt that this wasn't long term and that I hadn't done anything wrong, but you kept going, and you kept trying to do things your own way, and all along I kept calling for you, reaching for you, but you walked further and further away.

I couldn't figure it out.

I was so hurt.

But not as hurt as I was when I was strung up on the cross.

When I died for you.

But you forgot…you forgot the sacrifice I made for you because you graduated and got that degree, met new friends, got that job, and then met that man.

And yeah, he's gone now, but when you were with him and met him, he was your life, and I'm glad to have you back and glad to know you need Me now and to see you on your knees. I will be right there joining you.

There's no need for you to seek anything other than Me because, you see, I am the truth and the light.

I am God!

MY HAIR

Staying up late to get my hair pressed,

When tomorrow I have that early-morning test,

Holding my ears back and hearing that sizzle,

I can feel that Blue Magic drizzle.

Upset with momma for the pain of this hot iron so close to my head,

Not understanding what all the fuss is about.

Why I can't rock my Afro puffs?

Why I can't be who God made me to be?

And then it went from the pressing comb to Dark and Lovely.

The Dark and Lovely that left scars and pain,

And it never even did the job of straightening the roots,

When all I wanted was to accept the roots from which I came.

Who are you to blame,

Blame me for being aware

And not moved by the tactics and scare?

And not ashamed of who I am,

after the years of conditioning, I became that one

Who wore all the weave to disguise who she was,

The layers of tracks that fell down my back,

But then I started to seek the truth.

It became clear and evident that these products were damaging.

My hair was continuing to fall out.

It felt dead, and when I touched it, there was a story,

Wondering why I had chosen to murder the very strands that were on my head.

Could I be committed for such a violent and brutal attack?

And when would the repercussions of my decisions come back to haunt me?

Would I be accused of attempted murder in the first degree?

Who would be the judge and jury of this tragedy?

The hair that I've failed since the very beginning.

How I've changed the coils and the patterns and flows

Of the beautiful hair that laid upon my head.

And hearing the news that my ends were dead.

I WRITE

As much as I try, I can't.

No words will come out; no sound will even affect you.

So in order to reach you in a higher place at a higher level, I write.

I write to feel you, to hear you, and to soothe you…or you soothe me.

When my writing becomes ineffective, I sigh.

I talk to you with my hands, exploring your mind, exploring your thoughts and your feelings.

Hoping and praying that one day our language will be the same and without blame.

In the turmoil and despair, I had forgotten and so have you.

Forgotten what got us here in the first place.

How there was simplicity in the beginning, peace in the beginning,

Love in the beginning.

The beginning of you and I.

The first day I laid paper to pen and you spoke back to me.

The way you looked back at me and gave me power as I spoke the words on wrinkled-up paper.

Nearly empty ink pens.

Sometimes needing the lens to see you closer.

As my soul cried out to you, I felt closer and grew fonder of you.

I write because nothing or no one else understands me like you do.

You've shared and felt nearly all my pain.

I don't know how you've been able to sustain.

It seemed often that you would have to be part of my deepest despair.

But all of my writing seemed to be the repair.

I thank you for never judging me and allowing me to spill my love, anguish, and pain

On the corners of your creased pages.

I write to get back to me and you.

My very first love.

There for me through all of my pain.

CARPET RIDE

This won't be a carpet ride.

No, you see this thing called life,

It won't be gliding and subsiding up in the air

And through galaxies and stars without any despair.

This thing called life will hand you a share of challenges,

But be reminded you are more than a conqueror.

Allow those dim days to provide you with patience

In knowing that trouble doesn't last all the days of your life.

Sometimes you really do have to get up and fight

And not walk into that little dim light.

If you have to fall on your knees and pray to your Father,

I encourage you to do just that.

BOOK TITLE

Shifting through titles as if you are at a bookstore,

You rest on a title.

A title of my book, my story, as you try to figure out who I am.

And depending on the day you enter my life, your interpretation of my story can be skewed, wrong, untimely, or judgmental.

See, on Monday I was hit with the madness and mayhem of a tragic loss.

By Wednesday things were completely out of whack.

I had to put on a fake Friday smile and pretend that things were intact.

I stood at the altar on Sunday not because I'm perfect or righteous but because my week was full of turmoil and I had to say thank you for keeping me.

During that week several things were on display.

The lack of sincerity and understanding from some told a complete story,

Not to mention the judgment that others seemed to try to pass without knowing what I was battling.

But then I learned to not care about what they thought because it really didn't matter.

I knew who I was and whose I was and was completely comfortable in the skin I'm in.

So when you sift through, trying to pick my title,

Just know that to me it really doesn't matter.

My main goal is to reach higher and inspire others to live their potential and all their dreams.

SHE MATTERED

Another body bag.

Just because of a missed opportunity to brag.

You stole a life because your ego wouldn't allow you to hear no.

And who do you think you are that you can't be rejected?

So you decided to take this woman's life

And be a coward because your line just didn't suffice.

So many lives affected by your poor judgment,

But your judgment day will surely come.

The pain that you and your family will sustain,

The loss and turmoil her family has had to endure,

The poor example you've shown to other young men,

All because you received a no.

BATTERED AND BRUISED

I was bruised, battered. Hardly recognizable.

Black and blue and the pain that jolted through my body is indescribable from the pounding and pounding against my body.

Or so I thought against my body…it was all internal; it was an internal beating.

A savagely internal bleeding.

And I wondered why I always cried out when externally there was no sign of abuse.

My abuse was self-inflicted.

Constantly battering myself,

Hitting my head up against the wall countless times,

Struggling with the things that hurt me so,

Not realizing I was causing this battered body to be thrown about to and fro.

The constant bad decisions…the people I allowed around me.

And although I knew that this would lead to another scar or bruise, I continued to allow this savage beating upon me.

HIGH

I'm high on cloud nine,

Not high on crack or cocaine.

But statistically I could have fallen victim to floating on a crack-pipe high.

You see, the government infested our neighborhoods with crack cocaine, heroin, and PCP in hopes all our people would fade into…beep, beep, beep…no pulse.

In hopes that the craving would induce the desire to attack, kill, and destroy their closest counterpart.

This could have been me.

You see, statistically they say I shouldn't be educated and I certainly shouldn't be demonstrating and attempting to make preparations for a continued elevation of our young people.

Our young people who turn to a life of crime, thugging and killing for a petty dime bag.

Statistically, well, I don't wanna talk about it. Let's fix this statistic thing.

CONFUSED LOVE

I've haphazardly confused your emotions toward me as love.

You were so convincing with your words that I just knew it was real.

I was so blown away by your charismatic charm, white gleaming teeth, and one attractive face

I knew it was too good to be true; however, I waited for your call.

Waited for your return.

Waited on you, only to be disappointed.

Disappointed by your big ego.

But don't worry. I've finally let go.

I DON'T MIND

I don't mind.

I don't mind running your bath water and preparing your meals before you arrive home after a long, hard day at work. No, I don't mind.

I don't mind rubbing your neck and shoulders,

Massaging your body from head to toe.

Giving you that hour massage without the introductory fee of $39.99.

I don't mind surprising you by treating you to a night on the town.

I don't mind feeding you, and I certainly don't mind bathing you.

I don't mind watching SportsCenter on ESPN.

I'll even call customer service to order that DIRECTV Sunday Ticket for you.

I don't mind being what you need in the bedroom, providing you with all that you desire, and I don't mind keeping that discreetly between us.

I don't mind being seductive, intriguing, loving, sexy, and freaky with you.

I don't mind any of these things because I can rely on you to be my homie, my lover, and my friend.

You don't mind giving me my time and space to hang with the girls, and you don't mind that I'm a strong and resilient woman, yet loving, tender, and kind.

Because you don't mind all these things and you don't mind making me feel loved, special, and cared for, I don't mind stroking that ego when in fact I'm not stroking your ego at all.

I'm telling you exactly who you are and what you mean to me.

How unique of a man you are and how proud I am to have you on my arm.

Yes…I don't mind.

INVITE

I've invited you here.

It was an open invitation.

You received a written and verbal invite.

In your response I determined that you weren't completely sure about my invite.

In fact, you showed me several signs of your lack of interest, lack of patience, lack of affection, lack of respect.

However, my attraction and need for affection drew me in, and well, I did invite you in.

THANK GOD FOR MY DAYS

Kiss a girl, get a girl.

Tag—you're it!

Freeze!

Eeny, meeny, miny, mo!

Thank God for childlike imagination.

Imagination that allowed me and my friends to never miss PS3s and Xbox 360s—hell, our parents couldn't afford that anyway.

Thank God for the peace we felt by catching snowflakes on our tongues and feeling happy we'd caught the ice-cream man.

Thank God for mud pies and even raggedy park slides.

Thank God we didn't miss out on much…we caught lightning bugs in mason jars, and we were raised by our neighbors, aunts and uncles and grandparents, and of course our parents.

Thank God for all the love.

And now thank God that despite not being able to run and skip and play jump rope, I can still thank God.

JUST LIKE THAT

Just like that.

It was just like that that you received your wings.

Wings to take flight into the land of peace,

A quiet place that has true heights.

What a blessing it was to have had you in our lives.

Remembering your laughter and smiles provides such a source of gratitude to the Most High.

And for me to be blessed enough to have known you truly warms my soul.

In this remembrance of you, we will always cherish you.

THIS IS MY LIFE

This is my life.

I said, this is my life.

Hello, this is my life.

And I'm taking it back.

You tried to destroy me from the very beginning by tearing me down,

Trying to rip my fingers from the ladder on which I climbed.

Speaking negatively of me and against me as if the ancestors and the God in me could not rise.

All attempts to kill, destroy, and/or take from me will not go down.

I am a warrior and fighter, and if you check my record it consists of no losses and no knockouts.

You have pumped my adrenaline; as you focus on trying to destroy me, I am refueling and rebuilding.

There is nothing inside me but win.

As a matter of fact, I'm allergic to loss, and anything you toss this way with your anger, resentment, and hate will be intercepted.

This interception will be a ball that bounces back at you, so everything sent this way will come right back atcha.

Now as you sit there with that ball in your lap—that negative ball you tried to throw this way—just think about how I didn't play that.

WEB OF LIES

Somehow I've become entangled in this story full of lies.

The rumors and gossip that led to a number of good-byes.

Not sure how this web of destruction and lack of the correct information

Led to this level of defamation.

Inserting me in stories I never belonged.

And wondering why there was this long drawn-out story

That didn't make any sense.

And lacked all credibility and reasoning.

But you had to be spinning your wheels to comprehend how this could be real.

The lack of proof, the crossed eyes.

Even the source from which it came

Should have made you think, "Where's the proof?"

And the person who came to you was so aloof.

So the rumors and lies that you have passed

Should make you feel just as crazy as the one that initially surmised.

SEE YOU

I hear you, but I must watch you.

Keeping an eye on you to see if your actions match up to the words that come out of your mouth.

Confident that paying attention will avoid future distress.

Insistent on staying consistent and following my path.

Even knowing how hard it can be.

But trusting God to continue to be by my side.

Understanding and acknowledging my life's blessings.

Knowing that the pain I've sustained was building my character,

Increasing my faith,

Which will build my wealth,

Not just monetary wealth but the wealth and health necessary for continued breakthroughs,

Allowing myself to feel and love and even forgive.

So I'll continue to watch and see if your words are aligned with action.

And if they don't, be wise enough to pay attention to the signs.

BLOODSTAINED PAVEMENT

The bloodstained concrete left the daily reminder of hate, anger, and especially pain.

As if continued brutality and lack of care wasn't enough for all the recent years.

And lack of compassion for the hurt and those who felt betrayed.

The continued delays.

Delays to bring forth the murderer for fear of his life and that of the woman who wasn't his wife,

the lack of acknowledgment for taking a human life.

And you act baffled about protests and refusal to accept another lie as we've continued to watch you strip away our young men's lives and now more often our women.

This is becoming to be a familiar and painful reminder.

Class is continual in session in our homes.

Always keep your hands by your side.

Make no sudden or quick moves.

Don't even open your mouth to say a word.

It doesn't matter if you are being abused.

As we are continually used, violated, beat, and battered and not as they muse.

Nothing about this continued experience renders peace.

But it does make those who are tired want to grab their own piece.

For some that means their bullhorn.

For others it means reciprocating the violence ensued.

At some point this has to end.

No more excuses for the public sin.

PAIN IN HER EYES

The pain in her eyes said it all.

Unfortunately, no one paid close enough attention.

She always had so many around her.

People enjoyed the joy she evoked.

But so many of them needed to be stroked.

And eventually she felt choked.

Not willing to give so freely any longer.

Withholding more up front to see who really lasts.

No longer looking at the past.

Accepting things and moving on.

Replacing negative thoughts with positive memories.

Believing in knowing we all have a history.

Being completely happy and not part of any misery.

Because it really is true—misery loves company.

She can now admit she used to act a fool.

That pain of the past caused so much hindering in her growth.

But the moment she finally realized that her plan was greater,

She released those past demons.

And commenced to her dreaming.

Allowing peace and forgiveness to enter her spirit.

Then knowing that she had been delivered.

KINDRED SPIRITS

We were introduced, and all went well.

There was so much we shared in common, and things were swell.

We had love for the same things and aspired higher than most around us.

The trips we took and time we spent meant everything to me.

Our bond was stronger than any other I've ever had.

I didn't see that things were so bad.

That jealousy and envy had really set in.

And the love I thought you had for me was really fake.

It broke my heart to know the spirit I thought was kindred to mine

Was really waiting for things to fall apart all around me.

That the things you did behind me to deceive.

How you judged and belittled me to others.

The stories you made up to make yourself feel better.

I knew you had to feel the hurt you inflicted and how you knew you were wrong.

How heavily that must sit on your chest.

To know you had someone to care nonetheless and wish you nothing but the best.

I understand how the world evolves and that some people just can't go.

And as much as it hurt, I am happy to still have known you, and you will always remain a once-upon-a-time kindred spirit.

THE TRUTH

My love for you was so deep and strong.

In fact, I thought I found a good thing.

It was hard to believe that was all a joke.

The secrets and lies that later came out

Would leave me feeling hurt, angry, and betrayed.

Then God told me that love would be delayed.

Because there was so much more in the making of me.

So He had to push me into my true destiny.

Anytime your love for someone else is in competition with me,

I will surely make a way to force some space.

It was hard for a minute because I thought it was right.

However, I had to be real and admit you were a huge risk of flight.

As the great Maya Angelou so eloquently recites, "When someone shows you who they are, believe them the first time."

I have definitely learned some very tough lessons.

Be wise going forward, and receive all God's blessings.

PURPOSE

When I stepped into my purpose,

Releasing all fears and doubts,

Pursuing passionately and with belief that no obstacle will block my progress.

Believing that my life was intended for greatness,

A great peace and humbling feeling to be in his presence.

Creating, dreaming, and aspiring to continue to go higher.

I have felt nothing but a new power.

And I feel so inspired and will continue to aspire.

The path I'm on is one that brings the highest self-esteem.

The freedom to continuously dream.

To have hope that anything you want to do is attainable

And knowing I must continue to stay level headed so its sustainable.

Knowing that I am my biggest fan and I don't need anyone in the stands.

I can rise and applaud myself.

For remaining humble and true to me,

Having courage and vigor

Just to continue to pursue,

Pursue the things that pulled at my heart,

And that included my art,

My ability to put words together and tell a story.

Trusting the gifts I've been blessed with while sharing with the world what I've held within.

Feels so good pursuing passion and purpose, and I encourage you to do the same.

INGREDIENTS TO LIFE

Step one: Assemble love, grace, forgiveness, and hope.

Step two: Mix it together in one bowl and combine it to devote.

Devote to creating a new and more positive life.

It is simple to do when you've created a life with no strife.

Step three: Increase your faith; it helps to motivate.

Step four: After assembling and mixing all ingredients, do not hesitate.

It is time to move forward and create this new way.

You have just been supplied with all the ingredients to go on your day-to-day.

This is a recipe you may share to show your loved ones you care.

And the great thing is, it can be achieved when followed.

So lastly, fall on your knees and release that load.

You will no longer feel like you will explode or even implode.

This recipe will invoke peace.

And you will have life's increase.

THE AWARD GOES TO YOU

And the award goes to…you.

All of you.

Every one of you will get an award at the end of this night.

Because you have contributed to life.

Wouldn't that be ideal?

Wouldn't that bring on such an appeal?

To have everyone enthralled in your community, working with children and even the elderly?

Creating, inspiring, and thriving.

Wouldn't you like that announcement, that this award goes to you?

How many times have you seen someone in need?

And instead you've allowed them to continue to make a plea.

What will life look like for you?

If you received an award for every act of kindness, for every stand you made for humanity?

Without involving yourself or getting caught up in the insanity?

There's a lot to contribute.

So this award goes to you!

YOUR ASSUMPTIONS

Your assumptions are wrong.

I am not all that strong.

And the only reason you see this smile and my back standing tall

Is because I wasn't afraid to fall and then crawl.

Wasn't afraid to crawl and kneel

And request from the Highest my appeal

For forgiveness and asked of repentance.

A sincere and devoted approach to the One and Only whose presence I remain in.

Trying to contain myself, for I know this wouldn't have been possible without Him

And knowing how tough and grim this could have been.

But when I completely relied on Him and leaned not to my own understanding,

You would be shocked to know what He revealed in me.

A splendid and beautiful woman He said I would be,

Deleting the scenes and images that portrayed my broken heart

And replacing them with love for self and the truest form of transparency.

No longer feeling I had to disseminate charity,

Trying to fix and help everybody,

Concluding that I deserved more, and God said, "You won't have a choice but to wait,

Wait on what I've specially designed for you."

Make no assumption: I had to learn to sit back and hear, listen, and yes, wait,

But one thing I can say now is, it's so much easier when you don't see it as a delay.

So yes, your assumptions were wrong; I wasn't all that strong,

But I knew to Whom I belonged.

WITHDRAWAL

Making a withdrawal to take care of all the household needs.

Looking at the budget and projecting how long she will have to be on her knees.

Pleading to God to just intercede,

Make sure it all works out because she has kids to feed,

Bills to pay, and food to buy.

She is trying her hardest not to cry.

Things have been extremely tough since that man said good-bye.

The hope is that this withdrawal goes through—

Goes through without any form of delay

As she contemplates what items she can put on display

At the next yard sale,

To make ends meet until the next pay day.

MY TEARS

My tears reflect the light that shines brightly on my child.

The combination of hurtful and happy years has created a map on my face as the journey of motherhood has tested me.

I embrace each and every line on my face and choose to share those line lessons with other mommies.

You tend to seek other faces with those traced lines.

Others you can embrace and shed a tear with.

Some feeling challenged, tired, and weary

But committed to crying,

Crying out to God and praying for their children.

Those dried up tears that sit on your face so long it leaves this map.

The map of your journey that tells stories if you quiet long enough.

Touch her face, close your eyes, and trace those lines.

My tears.

You may have to shed a tear or two, but the story may just help you.

Allow your story to reach the masses without ever stepping foot into a class.

Don't even be distracted by the number of lines, and don't let it consume your mind or time.

Twenty-one years ago, I never knew how much more my love could grow.

How that son of mine means even more than the highest appraised dime.

Until I traced my own lines.

I close my eyes and remember what each line represents and thank God for this borrowed time.

From that first year when I learned about the date you'd arrive, to the last tear when I told you how proud I was to have you.

My tears.

PRAISE FOR KEYA'S WORK

"Keya's spoken word talent is such an art. She really does reach way down in the depths of her soul and find true words and situations to bring to life. I really appreciate what she does; it is so genuine and has blessed me in so many ways. Keep writing and sharing your most intimate inner thoughts. Your work is a blessing to many. There is no other like you."

—Culeta Hendricks, founder of Reprieve Spiritual Wellness

"Keya's poetry is truly inspiring. So much so that I asked her to perform a piece at my fortieth birthday celebration. Her pieces are liberating and thought provoking."

"Each time I hear her, it's a treat. What a phenomenal woman and poet she is!"

—Carmen Steward, president of Family Enrichment Support Center, St. Louis, Missouri

"Keya McCain is an artist that uses her spoken word as a vessel to empower women. The way she draws you in with her voice and tone speaks life into your situation. Every time I hear her poetry, I become a part of the next line. Keya's poetry carries you to a place of serenity and understanding. I am always grateful to be blessed by her words."

—Jarita Williams, educator/social-media manager of Jaritasociallyspeaking

"Keya's poetry is an intimate expression of love, pain, joy, and empowerment. It always lifts me up spiritually and mentally, embracing and comforting me emotionally. It is a fine example of powerful literature in every way!"

—Floyd Boykin Jr., poet, author, editor of SpokenVizions Magazine

"Keya's poetry is dynamic and empowering to all, especially women. I love that she speaks heart to heart! There aren't many poets out there doing what she does!"

—Tenille Rose Martin, sister friend

"Keya "Kinetic K" poetry evokes imaginative illusion awareness of experience or a specific emotional response detangling myths into reality. It's like her poetry is chosen, influential lyrics arranged for its meaning sound, and rhythm. A perfect song with lyrics that will uplift you, check you and or reflect your inner self. You can't help but listen in a subdued state."

---Belle Be, Visual Glass Artist/Model/Actress, Belle Be Proclaimed Arts

"While sitting, watching, listening, and feeling Keya speak, sharing such an eloquent piece of herself, I at that very moment saw myself in every word, every syllable, and every adjective! She has a gift of mesmerizing an audience. Her spoken word leaves one feeling uplifted, empowered, and at peace with her own sister, all her sisters, and ultimately herself. She has the ability to tell a story, share a testimony, and take people on a journey that some may never have known they wanted or needed to travel on! She has a gift that is like a rare jewel! She is a phenomenal woman indeed."

—Aretha McFall, sister-friend

"I always look to Keya's poetry whenever I need to be lifted or just need to read or hear things from a woman's perspective. She is very thoughtful and truthful and always gives her listeners very good insight. She is a very wonderful person, mother, and friend. I am so proud of her!"

—Kelvin Evans, professional musician and recording artist

This book is dedicated to myself for myself first. I thank God for giving me the will and strength to write and share. To forgive freely and openly. I dedicate this book to my son, who has always been my true motivation. To my dear uncle Prince, who is resting away physically but always in my heart; my dear friend and brother, Lydell Templeton (Rusty); my grandfather Sylvester Woolfolk, whom I loved dearly; my mother, Deborah Miller (one of my biggest fans); my dedicated and loyal friends and family; and my fans, who've cheered me on and attended shows and purchased this book. I am grateful to you all, and this book is dedicated to you.

Made in the USA
San Bernardino, CA
01 July 2016